# naturally *creative* candles

# naturally *creative* candles

### discover the craft
### of candle making
### and decorating using
### nature's bounty

## Letty Oates

**krause publications**

This book was designed and produced by

Quintet Publishing Limited

6 Blundell Street

London N7 9BH

CREATIVE DIRECTOR: **RICHARD DEWING**

ART DIRECTOR: **SILKE BRAUN**

DESIGNER: **SIMON BALLEY**

PROJECT EDITOR: **KATHY STEER**

EDITOR: **BARBARA CROXFORD**

PHOTOGRAPHER: **JON BOUCHIER**

STYLING: **LABEENA ISHAQUE**

Typeset in Great Britain by

Central Southern Typesetters, Eastbourne

Manufactured in Singapore by Pica Graphics

Printed in Singapore by

Star Standard Industries (Pte) Ltd

Please take particular care when lighting and burning candles

as they could be a fire hazard. Always make sure the candle

is secure and never leave a lit

candle unattended.

# contents

*The candle has been with us a very long time and, although no longer a necessity, is having a revival in interest. It is an art form in itself and in the atmosphere it can create.*

*Candles have been used in one form or other from earliest times to give light. Paintings on prehistoric caves and Egyptian tombs show the use of candles. David Constable in his book,* **Making Candles,** *says "The historian Pliny tells of candles in the first century AD being made either of pitch with a wick of flax, or molten wax into which a rush was dipped and the wax allowed to harden." The term candle is derived from the Latin* **Candere,** *which means to flicker or glitter.*

# intro d

*In Mediterranean countries, candles were made from oil and because the olive oil did not rise far up the wick, they were shaped flat like slippers. In North Europe where no natural oil was available, the poor used "farthing dips" or "rushlights" made by dipping thin sedges or split rush stems in tallow (animal fat) or beeswax.*

*Wealthy people used beeswax candles for themselves and tallow ones for their servants. The Romans used both tallow and wax, and both these materials remained in use until the mid-nineteenth century when a wide choice of fuels became available. Chemical research into animal fats resulted in the discovery of stearin which could be used to harden fats. This discovery meant that candles could be produced relatively cheaply and were a great improvement on tallow candles, which produced black smoke and a terrible stench when they burned.*

*Until a Frenchman called M. Cambaceres created the braided wick in 1852, there had been a problem with wicks not burning properly. This led to the manufacture of wick trimmers called snuffers. It was quite usual to snuff* candles every 30 minutes. The braided wick, with one thread drawn more tightly, would curve naturally and burn away to keep itself to its right length.

Joseph Morgan invented a candle making machine in 1834. This machine was capable of manufacturing fifteen hundred candles an hour. Two years after this, a palm oil substance was patented as an alternative to waxes. By the mid-nineteenth century, candle making companies owned coco-palm plantations in Sri-Lanka.

Candles have moved a long way from these humble beginnings, and are now used to create a pretty glow and to make a pleasing atmosphere. From the many projects created in this book, you will find that candles can be pretty

# u c t i o n

and fun, as well as enriching and enhancing a scene. There are candles for special occasions such as Thanksgiving, Christmas and weddings. There are wildly colorful candles, and there are the plain and elegant candles. We provide directions for making both the candles themselves and the containers in which they are displayed. Candles may be decorative in themselves, either painted or decorated with pressed flowers, pins, sequins, and beads. They may be made in layers with softer colored wax over a harder white wax. The softer wax can be sculpted or carved to reveal the contrasting wax underneath.

We show you how to make the best use of seasonal fruits, flowers, vegetables, and berries. Create both table settings and candles for all areas in the home and outside. Make use of a tree in the garden and use it for hanging lanterns. Collect items from the sea—shells, driftwood, beached starfish— and use them to make a warm evening setting. This book has been written to fill you with inspiration and I hope it does.

# MAKING
## *candles*

THERE ARE MANY WAYS IN WHICH TO MAKE CANDLES, FROM THE VERY SIMPLE ROLLED BEESWAX SHEETS TO

THE MORE COMPLICATED VARIATIONS USING SEVERAL COLORED WAXES IN ONE MOLD. HERE ARE A NUMBER

OF PROJECTS WITH CLEAR STEP–BY–STEP INSTRUCTIONS ON HOW TO MAKE CANDLES VERY SIMPLY.

BY USING THE MOST BASIC AND INEXPENSIVE TOOLS AND MATERIALS DESCRIBED IN THIS CHAPTER, YOU

CAN MAKE A VARIETY OF CANDLES FOR YOURSELF, AND FOR ALL YOUR FRIENDS AND FAMILY.

# materials and tools

You will need candle making equipment and tools before you begin to make your candles. However, they are inexpensive and easy to find in art and craft stores, or through mail order (see page 126). Some equipment you may already have at home in the kitchen, like a double boiler.

**❶ paraffin wax** is the most basic ingredient required for candle making. It is a by-product of the oil industry, produced through the refining of crude oil. Paraffin wax is odorless and colorless, and is mainly available in pellet form for making candles. It has a wide melting range between 105°–160°F. When the wax has melted, the result is a transparent thin liquid that looks like water. As it cools and starts to solidify, the wax becomes malleable and is therefore a good modeling material.

**❷ beeswax** is a wax that has been used for centuries and is the oldest type of wax known to man. It has a wonderful perfume and texture, and comes in many different variations of its natural color, from the lightest yellow to deep brown. It is also available in bleached white. Beeswax is often added in a small percentage to many candles as it increases the burning time of candles. Church candles have for centuries been made from beeswax. However, in modern times the average content of beeswax in a candle is more like 25 percent rather than 100 percent. It melts to a thick syrupy consistency, as it cools it also becomes quite malleable, but then becomes very sticky. Because of its stickiness, one should use a releasing agent to the mold first, if you are making a molded candle.

**beeswax sheets** are great for making the simple rolled candles. This just involves priming a wick and then rolling the wick tightly into the sheet. If the sheet seems stiff, it can be heated gently with a hair dryer or just placed against a heater for a few moments to make it softer.

**❸ wicks** It is important that you choose the right wick for the size and blend of waxes that you use for your candle. If the wick is too thick, the wick will burn and smoke; if the wick is too small, the flame will be much too small. It isn't the actual wick that burns, the wick just links up the vapor from the molten wax to the flame: it is the vapor that burns as the fuel is drawn up the wick.

The most popular of wicks are made of flat braided cotton, which are usually dipped in a chemical solution to retard burning. They are sold in 1/2 inch gradations, from 1/2–4 inches. The size of the wick depends on the size of the candle, for example you will need a 1 inch wick for a candle that's 1 inch in thickness.

Unless using dipped candles, you will probably have to prime the wick. This process is easy, simply melt some wax and leave the wick to soak for five minutes in the wax. Remove them,

place on a sheet of baking parchment or foil sheet and allow to dry.

**4 wax dye** is a coloring wax for candle making. It is available as dye discs in a huge range of colors. The amount of dye you need will vary according to the wax mixture and the size of the candle, generally 1lb wax will require a quarter of a disc, 2lb will require a half disc, and so on. Wax dyes can also be mixed as they are melted together. Do not over-dye the wax as it will reduce the glow of the candle. To achieve a true and bright color, the paraffin wax needs to have a little fat, stearin, mixed in.

**stearin** is used with paraffin wax to reduce its tendency to shrink, which in turn makes it easier to release from the mold, to give a good color when dyeing, and to stop the candle from dripping. A guideline to follow when using stearin is to use one part stearin to every ten parts of wax.

**mold seal** is a putty which is essential for sealing and making molds watertight. It is reusable and is used to secure the wick into place.

**heat source** is needed to heat the paraffin wax to a suitable temperature.

**5 scales** are needed to weigh out the materials to the exact measurements. Kitchen scales are fine for the job.

**6 double boiler** is a double saucepan used for melting wax over boiling water.

**7 dipping can** is a tall and thin vessel, used for holding hot wax. Ideal for making dipped candles, as it holds the hot wax deep enough to dip candles in. Alternatively a tall thin saucepan can be used. Dipping cans can be bought from craft stores and candle makers suppliers (see page 126).

**8 wicking needles** are used for threading wicks through candles and for piercing and threading wicks into molds. Can be used to secure a wick at the base of the mold, before pouring the wax into the mold. Available between 4 and 10 inches long.

**9 thermometer** measures the heat of the wax, a specialist wax thermometer is recommended. The thermometer should cover the scale between 100°–350°F.

**waxed paper/old baking sheet** are invaluable for pouring surplus wax onto while making candles.

**small kitchen weight** is useful for holding down a full mold, when it is in a water bath to stop it from floating.

**old wooden spoon** can be used for stirring the dye into the melted wax.

# before you start

Although candle making is a relatively easy craft, there are a few precautions that should be taken into consideration.

• Make sure the work area is clean and clear, and that you have everything assembled before starting candle making.

• Always keep the molds, saucepans, and other equipment clean, and wipe away any wax drips immediately.

• If you spill wax you will need to wait for it to dry before cleaning up. If wax spills onto cloth, it can be ironed away by placing brown paper on top of it and ironing.

• Wax burns like oil and will catch fire if raised to too high a temperature. Always use a thermometer as you cannot tell the heat of wax just by looking at it. Thermometers do not like being plunged into hot liquids, so always place the thermometer into the saucepan at the beginning of the heating process. This way you ensure an accurate reading.

• Never heat wax above 300°F.

Wax begins to smoke if it overheats. The heat source should be switched off immediately and the wax left to cool. If wax does catch fire DO NOT PUT WATER ON IT, this will spread the fire, either smother with a blanket or a saucepan lid.

• Keep unused wax clean. Put the wax in a container so it will not collect fluff or dust etc.

• Melted wax should never be poured down drains. Pour onto newspaper in a bowl, leave to dry, then put into the garbage. If there is a little excess wax left in a bowl, pour a drop of detergent and a little boiling hot water into the bowl and scrape the excess wax away. It should remove quite easily.

• Wax should not be left to set in a container with a wider base than top, as on heating the wax can spurt out and burn.

• When dyeing wax, remember that the color changes as it cools, generally it becomes a little lighter and more opaque.

**tea lights in frosted holders** These holders in different shades, give a wonderful soft glow when tea lights are placed inside them. The glass becomes semitransparent and reflects its colors onto the surrounding surface.

" *How* far that little candle throw his beams!"

SHAKESPEARE THE MERCHANT OF VENICE ACT 5, SC. 1, 1.24

# making beeswax candles

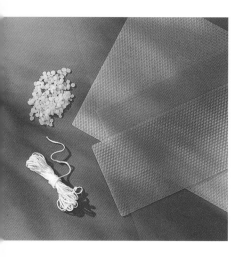

From the many uses of beeswax throughout the centuries, the most popular use has been for the production of candles. A special significance has been attached to beeswax candles by the Christian church since the 4th Century, representing the risen Christ. Altar candles are still required to contain a percentage of beeswax.

The candles shown in this project are made from beeswax sheets, which smell divine and look wonderful. They are the simplest types of candles to make. The wax sheets can be bought ready to roll and the only requirement is that they should be warm and pliable before you roll them. Although it isn't necessary to prime the wick, it is a good idea to do so, to prevent problems with the flame. This is a very simple process of dipping the wick into melted wax and allowing it to dry.

### you will need

**paraffin wax pellets**
**saucepan**
**wick**
**scissors**
**sheet of aluminum foil or**
**baking parchment**
**beeswax sheet**

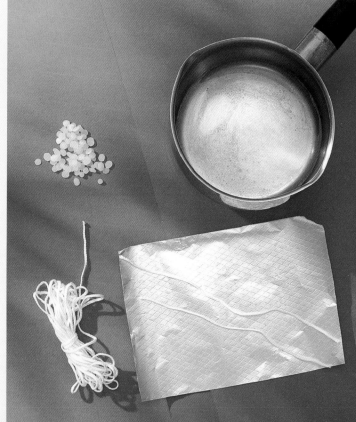

**one** To prime the wick, heat a small amount of wax pellets in a saucepan until melted. Cut off a suitable length of wick, this should protrude from the top of the candle by about 1 inch. Dip it into the hot wax and leave for about five minutes. Remove the wick and lay it on a sheet of aluminum foil or baking parchment and allow it to dry.

*making candles*

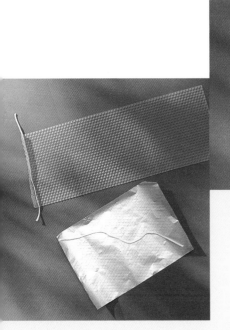

**three** Roll the wax around the wick, ensuring that the wick is kept tight as you roll. The wax should still be soft enough for you to push the edge into the candle to secure. Trim the wick with scissors if you need to.

**two** Warm up the beeswax sheet slightly, so that it will be malleable. Do this by using a hair dryer or placing it next to a warm heater for a few minutes. Line up the wick at one short end of the beeswax sheet and roll the edge over the wick.

# tapered candle

**you will need**

**beeswax sheet**

**craft knife**

**ruler**

**primed wick**

**spoon**

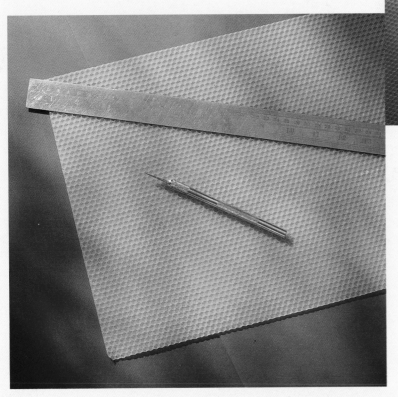

**one** Using a craft knife and ruler, cut the beeswax at an angle.

**two** Take the excess triangular wax piece and carefully line it up with the main piece. Cut along the bottom edge so that it fits onto the end of the main piece.

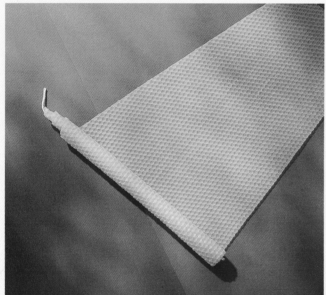

**three** Place the primed wick at one edge of the wax sheet and roll the sheet tightly around it, taking care to keep the bottom edge level.

**four** Once the main wax sheet is rolled, place the second piece against the candle. Push it into place with a hot spoon to secure it into place. Proceed to roll the rest of this piece around the candle and seal the end with the hot spoon.

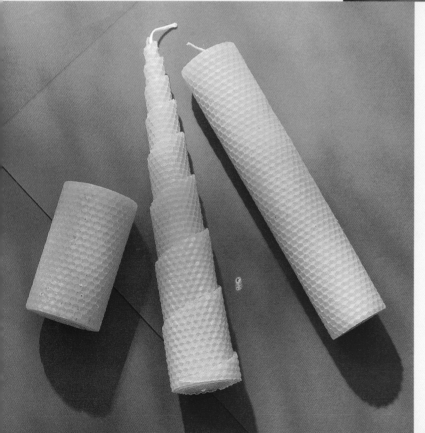

# making candles in molds

The most popular method of making candles is in molds. Molds come in many shapes and sizes, and are made from different materials including glass, plastic, rubber, and metal. The candles are made by pouring molten wax into a prepared container and allowing it to set.

The most basic of skills can produce a multitude of beautiful candles, from the simplest cylindrical mold to the most intricate floral embossed patterns of rubber molds. As candle wax has a tendency to pick up flaws from the surface of a mold, be sure to keep the molds absolutely clean between uses. Brush a tiny amount of cooking oil around the inside of the mold to ensure that tiny fragments of the previous wax are cleared up.

Paraffin wax pellets are recommended for the beginner. Beeswax pellets are more difficult to use because they are so sticky, therefore making it difficult to remove them from the mold without a releasing agent.

Stearin is added to the wax to prevent shrinkage and also allows the candle to be removed easily from the mold. You will notice that while the candle is setting in the mold, it shrinks at the open end, forming an open cavity. This end must be kept broken, by prodding it with a wicking needle and topping up the cavity with wax. However, do not fill above the original level, otherwise the wax will seep in between the candle and the mold, making it very difficult to remove.

### you will need

primed wick

baking parchment or aluminum foil

mold (in this case a plastic one)

wicking needle

mold seal

stearin (10% of the wax weight)

double boiler or container

wax dye

paraffin wax pellets

thermometer

tall container to use as a water bath

scissors

weight

cardboard

**two** Thread the primed wick through the closed end of the mold, pull the wick through so that it protrudes by about 1 inch. Now, make sure that end is watertight by pressing a generous amount of mold seal around the hole and wick.

**one** Prime the wick before you begin, by melting a little wax and immersing the wick in it for about five minutes. Remove the wick, lay it out on a sheet of baking parchment or aluminum foil and allow to dry.

**four** Melt the stearin in the double boiler over the heat (the amount you need is 10 percent of the wax used to make the candle); this will only take a few moments. When it has all dissolved, add the wax dye — for 7oz paraffin wax add 1/8 of a dye disc. Break the amount required into small pieces and stir until it has all melted.

**three** Pull the wick straight and taut, then carefully wind it around the wicking needle, which will act as an anchor for the wick, in case it falls into the wax.

**five** Add the paraffin wax pellets to the stearin and dye mixture, and allow it to melt. The mixture will have melted to a temperature of between 180°–199°F.

**six** Remove the double boiler from the heat and carefully pour the molten wax into the prepared mold. Wait one minute and then gently tap the side of the mold to release any air bubbles. Sit the mold in a container of cold water, weighing it down to stop it from floating, and allow to cool.

**seven** After about one hour a well will begin to form around the wick. Pierce around the wick with the wicking needle and top up the mold with 200°F temperature hot wax. Take care not to overfill from the original level. Allow the candle to set for a few hours. When it has set, the candle will slip out of the mold. Trim the wick with scissors. The base can be leveled off, by "ironing" it flat in a heated, empty saucepan.

**mantelpiece** A beautiful white mantelpiece holds a variety of altar candles among items that are often found on the

fireplace. The golden cubes with stars, hearts, and swirls cut from them are actually tea light holders. When the tea lights are

lit in these the effect is fantastic.

# using a rubber mold

The method for a rubber mold is almost identical to using a plastic mold, except that stearin isn't used. This is because the stearin will rot the rubber, therefore the dye is added to the melted wax, rather than adding the wax to the stearin and dye.

When rubber molds are bought, the top end will need to be pierced to allow the wick to go through. A wicking needle is used to thread a primed wick through the mold. Seal the hole with the wick using a mold seal to make it waterproof.

Most plastic molds have a base or platform to allow them to stand upright, whereas the rubber mold only has a lipped edge. This means that a collar or platform needs to be constructed to hold it vertical. The simplest way to do this is by taking a piece of card which is large enough to rest on the top of the water bath container. Draw around the open end of the mold onto the card and cut out. The mold will then slot in and be suspended in the water bath upright. This procedure is shown on pages 36 and 37.

## other molds

Many objects can be used as alternatives to the more traditional mold made of rubber, plastic, glass, and metal. For example, sea shells with large cavities can be used, not only to mold the candles in to be removed, but also as cases for the candles. Using this same principle, coconut shells and other larger nut shells can have candles set into them.

Old tins, look amazing when set with candles. Take inspiration from Hindu and Jewish prayer times and set candles in a wide variety of glass containers, including jam jars, drinking glasses, frosted jars, and wide-necked bottles.

Sand is fantastic to use as a mold. The sand has to be just damp and a well made in it before the molten wax is poured in. Once the candle is removed from the sand, with sand grains stuck on the candle, the effect is wonderful. However, remember when using sand as a mold, the temperature of the wax must be very high and the sand cannot be too damp. If the wax is too cool and the sand too damp, the wax won't penetrate and there will be no sand grains left on the candle surface when you remove it.

To make floating candles, cookie cutters are ideal. Use aluminum foil as a base and place the cookie cutter onto the foil. Seal the edges well with mold seal to ensure that the edges are waterproof and the molten wax will not escape.

In fact, anything that will withstand the heat of the molten wax will suffice as a candle mold, from heavy plastic trays found in some candy boxes, to sturdy yogurt pots and egg cups.

# making dipped candles

**you will need**

deep metal dipping can

large saucepan

stearin

wax dye

paraffin wax pellets

thermometer

24 inch length of primed wick, to make one pair of candles

long rod or hook to hang drying candles

sharp knife or scissors

*The method for making dipped candles is again extremely simple. It involves dipping a doubled-over length of wick into a tall container of molten wax. The candles are made as a pair, if the wick is doubled over, so that two are made simultaneously. They can be of any height, but are generally tall and tapered. Layer upon layer of wax is then added each time the wick is dipped.*

*These candles can be made in one color or they can be made as white candles and then overdipped. To overdip, a little wax and dye are melted together and then poured into a deep saucepan of boiling hot water. By holding the candles by the wick and gently dipping them into the water and wax they will become coated in the color, redipping for a more intensive color. Overdipped candles have a stronger color than solid color candles.*

*Striped candles can be made by overdipping. For example, to make a candle with five bands of different colors, you will need five saucepans of water with different colored wax floating on top of them. Dip the candle into the lightest color up to the wick, twice, then allow it to dry. Dip it twice into the next color but only part way up the candle and allow to dry. Repeat this process until all the colors have been used and the candle has a stripy effect.*

*However, to make simple dipped candles:*

**one** Put the dipping can into the saucepan and fill the saucepan with water. Bring the water to a boil. Heat the stearin in the dipping can and add the wax dye. Once these have completely melted, add the paraffin wax pellets. Heat the temperature to a steady 160°F. The dipping can should be filled with wax almost to the top.

**two** Holding the length of wick in the middle, submerge either end into the wax, leaving only a little wick uncovered at the top. Leave in the wax for 3–4 seconds and then remove. Do this in one movement, ensuring that the wick ends don't touch each other, otherwise they might stick together.

**three** Leave the candles to cool for 3–4 minutes. Hang up onto a hook or a rod for this duration. Repeat this dipping and cooling process until the candles are of the required thickness. Keep the temperature of the wax at a constant 160°F for up to thirty dips.

**four** For the final dip, heat the wax to 180°F and dip the pair of candles into the molten wax twice for at least three seconds, allowing them to cool for a minute in between dips. This will give a smooth and even finish. Allow the pair of candles to cool. Carefully trim the bases so they are flat, then trim the wicks to ½ inch and set for at least one hour before using.

**candles in a box** This box filled with rolled candles make a lovely present. The eau de nil distressed box was an old soap

box in which the candles fitted perfectly, and matched well with the muted lilac, blue, and green shades. The box was lined

with a bright blue taffeta fabric, which sets off all the colors wonderfully.

"*I shall light a candle of understanding in thine heart, which shall not be put out.*"

**II ESDRAS** CH. 14, v. 25

# hand molding candles

Warm wax is very workable as it is soft and malleable. Therefore, dipped candles that have just been made are perfect for hand molding into a number of different shapes. Remember when working with candles this way to keep the wax warm and in a malleable state. Before you begin to hand mold your candle, carefully test the candle to see if the wax is soft enough by gently bending it into an "S" shape, if it does so easily, then you can start.

If work becomes difficult, don't force the wax to twist or turn, simply redip the candle for about three or four seconds in molten wax at a temperature of 160°F. Leave the candle for about 30 seconds before you start working it again.

## rolling and twisting candles

**you will need**

pair of freshly dipped candles
knife or scissors
rolling pin

Cut the wick to separate the candles. Roll out and gently flatten each candle using a rolling pin on a clean, flat work surface, keeping the base round, as this has to fit into the candlestick or holder. Roll until it is about 1/4 inch thick.

Holding the base in one hand and the top wick end in the other, pull the candle upwards, twisting as you do so with your thumb and index finger gently easing it into a twisted shape. Trim the wick to 1/2 inch and allow the candle to cool for at least one hour before burning.

## braiding candles

**you will need**

three freshly made dipped candles
hook or rod to hang the candles
knife
scissors

Redip the three candles for three seconds. Tie all three candles together by their wicks and hang them from a hook so that the tops of all three candles are level with each other.

Begin to braid the candles together. Taking the left hand candle, pass it over the middle, then take the right hand candle and pass that over the middle. Continue this process until you reach the end.

When you have completed the braid, finish off by squeezing the ends together, to form a round base that will fit into a candlestick or holder. With a knife, flatten the base of the candle so it can stand up. Trim the wicks to about 1/2 inch and allow to cool for at least one hour before burning.

# stripy CONE candle

*This elegant, cone shaped candle is easy to make as long as the temperatures of the wax are high enough when pouring the layers into the mold. When all the layers have been poured into the mold, immediately submerge the whole mold in cold water and allow the wax to set for about two hours.*

**you will need**

**rigid plastic cone mold, with base**

**wicking needle**

**primed wick**

**mold seal**

**two double boilers**

**stearin**

**yellow and blue dye discs**

**paraffin wax pellets**

**thermometer**

**cold water bath, a basin, jug or deep bowl**

**scissors**

**one** Prepare the mold, by threading the primed wick through the hole at the base and securing it at that end with mold seal. At the open end of the mold tie the remaining wick to the wicking needle.

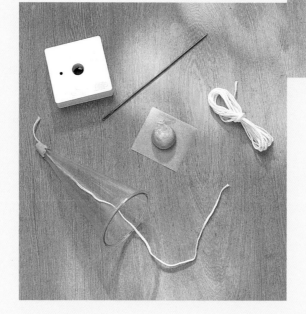

**two** Melt two batches of stearin, putting yellow dye in one and blue dye in the other, when the dye discs and the stearin have melted completely, add the wax to both mixtures and melt, until they reach a temperature of 350°F.

**four** When the first layer has set to the right texture, poke tiny holes into the wax using the needle around the wick. Then pour in the hot yellow wax, again fill the mold up to another third, so now the mold is filled to ⅔ of its capacity. Allow to set until it is rubbery to the touch.

**three** Starting with the blue dyed wax, fill the mold up to ⅓ of its capacity. Allow the wax to set for 15–20 minutes, or until it is rubbery to the touch.

**five** Poke tiny holes around the wick and pour in the final layer of blue wax, ensuring that the wax is at 350°F. Submerge the mold into a cold water bath and allow to set. Fill up the mold with wax as necessary.

**six** When the candle has set, tap the sides of the mold and carefully pull the candle out. Trim the wick to about ½ inch and stand the candle in an empty, warm saucepan so that the base is level.

"*Let there be light!*"

J. MARRIOT (C.1813).

# different candle effects

As you become more experienced and confident with your candle making techniques, you may wish to extend your basic techniques to encompass a whole variety of unusual methods and finishes.

Many different effects are the result of experimenting with the most basic of techniques. For instance, if you run out of one color of wax when filling a mold, then when you heat some more wax it may be a slightly different color when you finish filling the mold. This will give an excellent two tone layered effect to the finished candle.

This is the way in which many multi-colored candles are made, by basically pouring different colored waxes into the mold in layers. Each layer of wax should be quite cool and almost set before you add the next layer. If you move the mold around, so that it stands at various angles for each layer, this too can create varying effects.

Another technique is dyeing the wax while in the mold. Use dip and carve wax for this purpose. Break up small pieces of wax with a sharp knife as it can be difficult to break. Place the pieces into a mold, which has already been prepared with a primed wick. Melt wax and stearin together, without any dye in the mixture, until it reaches a temperature of 260°F. Pour over the wax chunks. Immediately spoon in drops of hot, just melted wax dye. The dye will then distribute itself around the mold in a swirly pattern. Have a cold water bath ready and carefully place the mold into the water to stop the dye from spreading any further. If you do not place the mold in the water bath when the dyes have swirled, they will slowly begin to lose definition as time passes.

Ice candles have an interesting finish, they are made by pouring hot wax over chunks of ice. As the wax sets, cavities are formed by the ice all over the candle. However, to prevent any water getting trapped next to the wick, a thin candle is placed in the center of the mold, secured with mold seal.

The spectrawax candles pictured opposite are made by using minute slices of different colored waxes, which have been embedded in a mold. A much simpler form of this is called a Bull's Eye candle. First, a candle is overdipped three or four times in strong contrasting colored waxes, then the wick is pulled out and removed. The candle is sliced quite thinly and a plastic mold is lined with these pieces, secured into place with tiny blobs of wax glue. A wax and stearin mixture is poured into the mold, being careful not to go over the lined sides of the mold. It is placed in a cool water bath and allowed to cool. As it cools, the candle is topped up and the cavity forms. When the candle has been removed from the mold, it is ironed off and smoothed, by quickly placing it in a warm pan. Alternatively, the surface is polished with mineral spirit.

# making scented candles

*Scented candles create a fabulous atmosphere when they burn, giving off wonderful aromas. Scented oils are available especially for scenting candles, obtainable in most candle stores. You can also use essential oils, known for their therapeutic qualities, for example, lavender and sandalwood promote feelings of calmness.*

*Scented candles can be made in different ways: the wick can be scented, while you are priming it. Add a few drops of scented oil to the molten wax and leave the wick in the mixture for 20 minutes. Another way is to stir fresh and dried herbs and flowers into the molten wax and stearin. Keep the wax at a temperature of 180°F, and leave for 45 minutes. Remove the herbs if you wish before making the candles.*

*Scented oils can damage plastic molds, so use rubber or glass molds. If you do use a rubber mold, do not use stearin in the wax mixture as this tends to rot the rubber.*

**you will need**

primed wick and wicking needle

rubber mold and cardboard collar (see page 25)

mold seal

tall container to use as a water bath

double boiler

paraffin wax pellets

wax dye

thermometer

scented oil

spoon

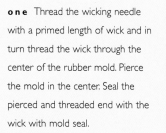

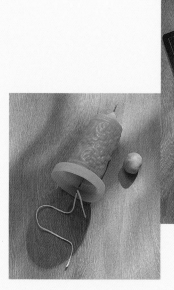

**one** Thread the wicking needle with a primed length of wick and in turn thread the wick through the center of the rubber mold. Pierce the mold in the center. Seal the pierced and threaded end with the wick with mold seal.

**two** Push the rubber mold into the cardboard collar, so that the open end is aligned to the collar.

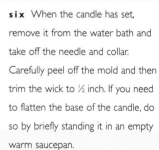

**three** Place the collar and mold in a tall upright container, so that the collar rests against the rim of the container. Secure the wick at the open end, by winding it around the wicking needle.

**six** When the candle has set, remove it from the water bath and take off the needle and collar. Carefully peel off the mold and then trim the wick to ½ inch. If you need to flatten the base of the candle, do so by briefly standing it in an empty warm saucepan.

**five** Pour the molten wax and scent mixture into the prepared mold. Fill the container that the mold is resting in with cold water, then allow the candle to set for about one hour. As a dip forms in the center of the opening, prick it with the wicking needle and pour in more wax to fill the hollow. Allow to cool for a few hours.

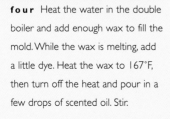

**four** Heat the water in the double boiler and add enough wax to fill the mold. While the wax is melting, add a little dye. Heat the wax to 167°F, then turn off the heat and pour in a few drops of scented oil. Stir.

*making candles*

# making embossed candles

*Although embossing can be done with bought rubber molds, it is always fun to discover different ways of embossing candles. Here, a regular plastic mold has been lined with a sheet of corrugated cardboard, which when removed gives a ridged surface to the candle.*

### you will need

**double boiler**

**stearin (10% of the wax content)**

**wax dye**

**paraffin wax pellets**

**thermometer**

**square plastic candle mold**

**corrugated or ridged card**

**primed wick**

**wicking needle**

**mold seal**

**scissors**

**two** While the wax is melting prepare the mold. Cut a piece of corrugated card to fit the inside of the mold quite tightly. Fold it into place, with the corrugated side facing inward.

**one** Pour boiling water into the double boiler. Melt the stearin and wax dye in the top compartment of the boiler. Add the wax pellets and melt to a temperature between 180°–199°F.

**three** Thread the primed wick through the wick hole. Secure at the hole end with a generous amount of mold seal and at the other open end with the wicking needle.

**five** After 3–4 hours, when the candle has set, remove the card with the wax encased in it from the plastic mold. Tap the sides of the mold at first and pull at the card, which will come away from the sides of the mold.

**six** When removed from the mold, cut and peel the card away from the candle. You will find that the card may leave layers of paper on the wax, giving the candle a textured look.

**four** When the wax has reached the correct temperature, pour into the prepared mold and allow to set for one hour. Prick the open end and pour in more hot wax as necessary.

# DECORATING *candles*

THERE ARE A MULTITUDE OF UNUSUAL AND EXCITING WAYS IN WHICH TO DECORATE CANDLES, EITHER

USING NATURAL FORMS THEMSELVES OR USING THEM AS INSPIRATION FOR PATTERNS AND APPLIED

DECORATION. INCLUDED ARE DECORATED CANDLES WHICH CAN BE USED AS SPECIAL GIFTS FOR MOTHER'S

DAY, VALENTINE'S DAY, CHRISTMAS, AND BIRTHDAYS. MANY OF THE PROJECTS CAN BE ADAPTED TO VARIOUS

OCCASIONS. FOR EXAMPLE, THE TECHNIQUE USED FOR THE HAND PAINTED PROJECT DEPICTING A PRETTY

IVY PATTERN COULD BE USED TO PAINT VALENTINE HEARTS OR CHRISTMAS SNOW FLAKES. IN THE CARVED

CANDLE SECTION WHERE A LEAF PATTERN IS USED, YOU CAN CHOOSE A DESIGN TO SUIT THE OCCASION.

SOMETIMES THE DECORATIONS CAN BECOME GIFTS, SUCH AS A BUNCH OF CANDLES TIED WITH A WIRED

RIBBON AND A PIECE OF LAVENDER. CHOOSE THE EMBELLISHMENT TO MATCH THE RECIPIENT – GIVE A

BUNCH OF CANDLES DECORATED WITH CHILES TO A KEEN COOK. HOWEVER YOU CHOOSE TO DECORATE

YOUR CANDLES, THIS CHAPTER IS FULL OF IDEAS TO START YOU OFF.

# shells and pebbles candles

*The use of natural materials for decorating is especially satisfying when the items being used are found. A great way to remember a vacation is to use the tiny pebbles and shells found on the beach.*

**you will need**

**tiny pebbles, shells or a mixture of both**

**thick candle, about 2¹/4 inch diameter**

**cutting tool with finest (No. 1) blade**

**paraffin wax pellets**

**saucepan**

**spoon**

**one** Using the cutting tool, mark or make small gouges evenly round the candle in the place where you want to position the shells and pebbles.

**two** Select light, small pebbles and shells from your collection, making sure they are clean and dry.

**three** Take a shell or pebble and hold it over one of the places you previously marked. Mark around the outside of it with the cutting tool. Remove the shell or pebble and gouge out enough wax so the shell or pebble will stay in it, but still stand out from the surface of the candle.

**four** Repeat step three with all the shells and pebbles until the candle is covered with them.

**five** Melt the wax pellets in a saucepan. Then, holding the candle by the wick, dip it into the hot wax. If you miss sections, use the spoon to pour the wax over these areas. The melted wax will help to hold the shells and pebbles in place.

**shell-embedded candles** These candles were decorated by scoring out wax and embedding tiny shells and pebbles

into the holes. The shells and pebbles secured by pouring hot wax over them. They look well placed in a sea-themed

surrounding like a bathroom. Pour tiny drops of scented oil around the wick and light them while you bathe.

"*Bell, book, and candle shall not drive me back, when gold and silver becks me to come on.*"

**SHAKESPEARE** KING JOHN ACT 3 SC. 3, l.12

# carved candles

*For this project the best candles to choose are those which have been overdipped (see page 22), that is a smooth white or cream colored candle which has then been dipped into a colored wax. This enables you to carve through the top wax layer to reveal the white candle underneath. Carving is a simple technique but you may need some practice with carving out more intricate designs.*

**you will need**

pencil and paper

pen or skewer

cutting tool with the finest (No. 1) blade

dipped candle

**one** Draw your design onto paper; as the design has to be seen in three dimension, a simple pattern is best.

**two** Using a pen or skewer, copy the design onto the candle. At this stage only press lightly in case you make a mistake.

**four** On the larger carved
sections, be careful not to lift off too
much of the colored wax by holding
it down with the tip of your finger as
you carve.

**three** Using the cutting tool,
carefully carve the design out of the
candle, removing the darker color to
reveal the white wax underneath.

# hand painted candles

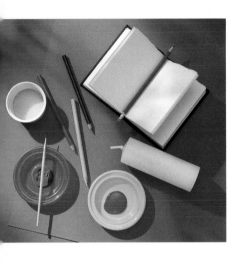

*Painted candles may be as simple as an overall dot pattern or as complex as the ivy pattern shown here. It is an easy way of personalizing a candle and making, for example, a birthday present or a moving house gift with perhaps the owner's new house painted on the candle. For the paint to adhere to the wax a few drops of dishwashing detergent should be added to the paint.*

**you will need**

**pencil and paper**

**colored pencils**

**acrylic paints**

**dishwashing detergent**

**natural colored candle**

**fine paintbrush**

**one** Draw and color in your design onto paper so that you have a guide to follow.

**two** Select your acrylic colors. Mix each color with a drop of detergent.

**three** Paint the design onto the candle. For this ivy leaf design (see page 123), mix the colors on the candle so that one color blends into another creating the look of autumn leaves.

# gilt patterned candles

By coating a candle in a different substance, you can create a new surface to emboss or score, and make an interesting pattern. In this project a dark blue colored candle has been covered in a gilt cream. Patterns are scored through the gold revealing the blue underneath and resulting in a dazzling effect.

### you will need

**gold gilt wax**

**large or small colored candles**

**soft cloth**

**pencil**

**metal skewer**

**two** Apply a second layer of gilt, ensuring that the whole of the candle is completely covered.

**one** Apply gold gilt wax to the candle using a soft cloth. Allow it to dry – this takes about 30 minutes.

**three** Mark a pattern on the candle with a pencil. Using a skewer, score out the marks through the gold to reveal the different candle color underneath.

# beaded candles

*Beads and sequins can be anchored into candles using pins. Because candles are a soft surface, it is easy to push pins into them. Choose tiny rocaille beads and sparkling sequins to create rich, ornate, and jewel-like candles. Before lighting this candle, remove all pins, beads, and sequins as they may catch fire.*

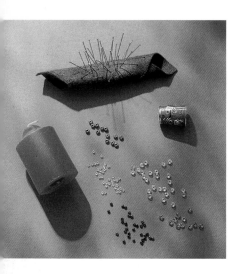

**you will need**

**rocaille beads and sequins**

**short pins**

**candles**

**thimble**

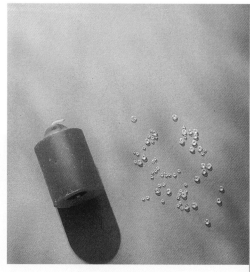

**one** Select the shape, size and color of the beads and sequins. Choose colors to complement the candle you are using.

**two** Thread the beads and sequins onto the pins.

**three** Gently push the pins into the candles, evenly spacing them. You may need to wear a thimble to do this.

# ribbon-wrapped candles

*A very easy way of decorating candles is to wrap them in ribbon. Make your own by cutting and fraying fabric or buy from the great variety available in stores today. The ribbon may be painted or decorated with beads or buttons. Before lighting these candles, remove the ribbon and sequins as they may catch fire.*

**you will need**

**selection of ribbons**

**beeswax candles**

**pins**

**raffia**

**leaf-shaped sequins**

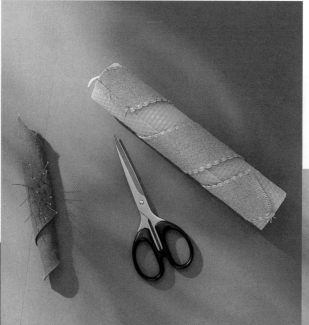

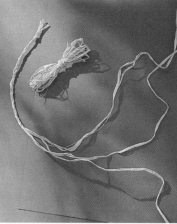

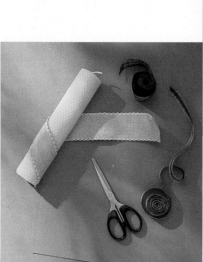

**one** Wind the chosen ribbon around the candle, then cut it to the right size.

**two** Wrap the candle in the ribbon again, this time carefully pinning it into place.

**three** Cut three pieces of raffia to the same length, long enough to wind around the candle when braided. Braid them together.

**five** Pin leaf-shaped sequins onto
the candle.

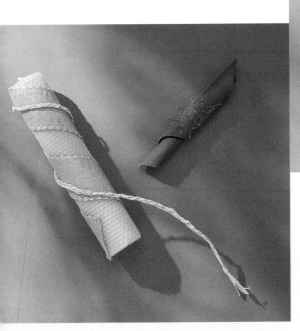

**four** Pin the braided raffia into
place on top of the ribbon or
between the ribbon spiral.

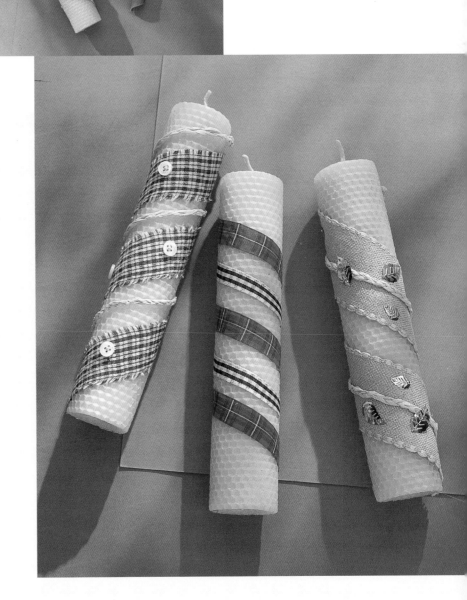

# chiles and lavender candles

*Dried fruits, flowers, or vegetables make very pretty candle decorations. If you dry your own, they are an inexpensive way of decorating candles.*

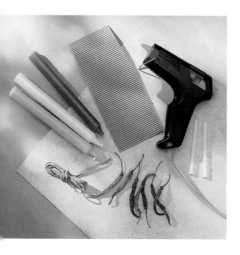

**you will need**

**corrugated card**
**dried chiles**
**glue gun**
**three colored candles**
**gold cord**

**two** Using a glue gun, glue the dried chiles around the card.

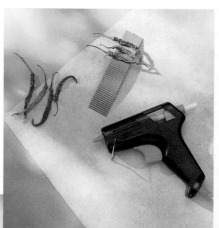

**three** Wrap the chiles and card around the candles then tie with gold cord.

**one** Cut out a strip of corrugated card long enough to fit around a bundle of candles.

## you will need

**several long, thin candles**

**elastic bands**

**dried lavender**

**scissors**

**wired ribbon**

**one** Hold the candles together with elastic bands. Cut the stems off the lavender.

**two** Push the shortened lavender under one of the elastic bands to hold in position.

**four** Alternatively, leave the lavender stems long before attaching to the candles.

**three** Wrap wired ribbon around the lavender and candles, and make a large bow.

**beeswax shaker candles** These beeswax candles have been gift wrapped with simple, country style ribbons, buttons, and raffia, to achieve a strong Shaker

look. The candle on the right has been wound with two contrasting gingham ribbons. The candle in the center has a frayed gingham fabric strip, with pearl shirt

buttons sewn onto it, wrapped around with a length of braided raffia. The candle on the left is shown as a project on page 50.

"*He hangs in shades the orange bright,*
*Like golden lamps in a green night.*"

A. MARVELL "BERMUDAS" (C. 1653)

# leaf-wrapped ribbon candles

*Green leaves look very fresh against ivory colored candles. The other two materials used to decorate this candle are metallic ribbon and foil leaves cut from a copper foil sheet. It will look more effective if the foil leaves are the same size. Before lighting these candles remove the leaves and ribbon as they may catch fire.*

**three** Cut leaves from the copper foil and emboss using a pencil.

**you will need**

- large green leaves
- thick ivory or natural colored candle
- elastic band
- metallic ribbon
- scissors
- copper foil sheet
- pencil
- glue
- fine paintbrush
- pins

**two** Cut a length of ribbon to fit around the candle.

**four** Using a paintbrush, glue the copper leaves onto the ribbon. Wrap the ribbon round the candle and secure tightly with pins.

**one** Wrap the large leaves around the candle and secure tightly with an elastic band.

# leaf-wrapped candle

**one** Wrap the stem of the leaves around the candle and then secure with tape.

**you will need**

stem of leaves

thick ivory or natural colored candle

clear adhesive tape

gold string

**two** Wind the gold string around the candle on top of the leaves, securing them in place. Carefully remove the tape.

*decorating candles*

**61**

# paper stars candle

These translucent looking stars are made out of handmade paper, cut into star and moon shapes. They are held in place by carefully heating a spoon in boiling water then placing the shapes on the candle and melting them into position with the spoon.

Before lighting this candle, remove the paper stars. They are easy to peel off.

**you will need**

**natural handmade paper**

**soft sharp pencil**

**cutting mat**

**craft knife or scissors**

**spoon**

**selection of tiny gold paper stars**

**thick white candle**

**two** Place the paper onto the cutting mat and carefully cut out the star and moon shapes, using long and smooth strokes with the knife to avoid jagged and torn edges.

**one** Draw star and moon shapes onto the handmade paper with a soft sharp pencil.

**three** Heat the back of the spoon in a bowl of boiling hot water, by dipping the spoon into the water for a few seconds and then drying it.

**four** Place the paper and gold stars and moons individually onto the candle, melting them into position with the hot spoon. The spoon will heat up the wax of the candle and make the paper shape adhere to the wax. You will need to reheat the spoon occasionally.

# pressed leaf candle

*To preserve the wonderful colors of autumn leaves, simply press them and then use to decorate plain church candles. Varnishing the leaves when they have dried will preserve them. This candle will look stunning by itself on the windowsill in the fall.*

*Before lighting this candle, remove the leaves. They are extremely easy to peel off.*

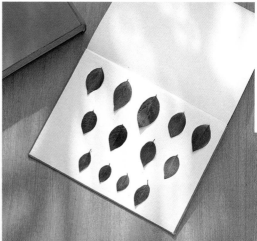

**you will need**

**selection of fresh leaves**

**flower press or heavy books**

**plain church candle or smooth sided pillar candle**

**clear matt or satin finish varnish**

**paintbrush**

**two** Place, undisturbed, in a warm dry place for about a week; by this time the leaves should be pressed completely flat. Carefully remove the leaves from the press or the book, ensuring that the surfaces are dust free and clean.

**one** Place the leaves between the blotting sheets of a flower press and screw it together. If you are using heavy books, place the flowers in between the pages of one book and then weight it down with the other books on top.

**four** Leave the candle in a dust free place to dry for about six hours. Apply a final coat of varnish to seal the leaves in place.

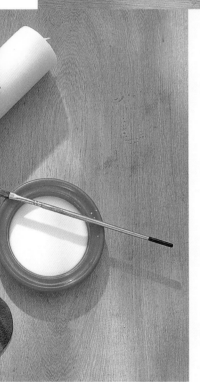

**three** Apply a thin coat of varnish to the surface of the candle. Allow to dry for 15–20 minutes, until it is sticky to the touch. Press the leaves onto the sticky surface, pressing each individual leaf down gently to ensure that it has adhered to the candle.

# DECORATIONS
## *and displays*

CANDLES ARE VERY OFTEN USED AS TABLE CENTERPIECES AND IN DISPLAYS FOR CELEBRATIONS AND SPECIAL

OCCASIONS. FROM THE ROMANTIC CANDLE-LIT DINNER FOR TWO TO THE FESTIVITIES OF CHRISTMAS TIME,

CANDLES PLAY A LARGE PART IN DECORATING THE TABLE AND CREATING A WONDERFUL ATMOSPHERE. THIS

CHAPTER SUGGESTS WAYS TO USE CANDLES TO CREATE THE PERFECT ATMOSPHERIC MOOD TO SUIT EVERY

OCCASION – THANKSGIVING, CHRISTMAS, WEDDINGS, ROMANTIC DINNERS, HALLOWEEN.

THE MOST UNUSUAL ITEMS MAY BE USED TO CREATE ATMOSPHERE, FOR EXAMPLE REAL PEARS CAN BE

RUBBED WITH A GOLD WAX TO GIVE A SHEEN AND THEN MIXED WITH GLEAMING GOLD, SILVER, OR OTHER

METALLIC CANDLESTICKS WITH A TRAIL OF IVY TO CREATE AN ATMOSPHERE OF OPULENCE. A GLASS CAKE

STAND WITH VARIOUS WHITE CANDLES, DECORATED WITH SPECIAL SILVER CANDLES, SILK, RIBBONS, AND

LILIES FOR A ROMANTIC WEDDING SETTING. OUTSIDE ON A COLD HALLOWEEN EVENING, PUMPKIN

LANTERNS MAY BE PERCHED ON A STEP LADDER AND SURROUNDED WITH BASKETS OF SEASONAL FRUIT.

# romantic dinner<sub>for two centerpiece</sub>

*The ubiquitous rose is the perfect flower for a candle and floral display for an intimate dinner table. The display is romantic, with its profusion of pink and red roses, and same colored candles.*

**you will need**

**florist wire**

**four pink spiral candles**

**one longer pink candle**

**five floral foam rounds**

**pump spray container of water or watering can**

**selection of pink and red roses**

**pink wired ribbon**

**dressmaker pins**

**t w o** Attach the candle to the center of the floral foam round by pushing the candle base and wire firmly into the floral foam. Ensure that the candle is standing upright and not at an angle.

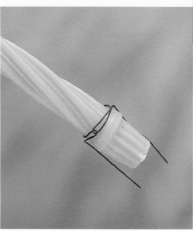

**o n e** Wind the florist wire around the base of a candle, winding off so that the wire ends are pointing down at two points.

**five** Before covering the ring in flowers, cover most of the floral foam with leaves taken from the rose stems.

**four** Once the candles are in position, spray the floral foam with water until it is quite wet. Although not soaking, it should be very damp to touch.

**three** Attach the florist wire to the remaining candles in the same way, then attach each candle to each individual floral foam round.

**six** Using the fuller pink flowers first, cut the stems to about 3 inches, with the end at a slight angle. Concentrating initially on the actual base of the ring and the candle base, start putting the rose heads into the floral foam. Keep the flower heads as close to each other as possible to create a tight floral ring.

**s e v e n** Trim the stems off the red roses and place the occasional one into the arrangement to add another color to the display.

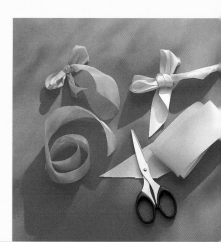

**n i n e** Pin the wired ribbon bows around the floral foam ring. The actual positioning of the bows will depend upon the positioning of the flower heads.

**e i g h t** Once the fuller flowers have been attached, trim the smaller pink roses, filling in the floral foam as much as possible.

**ten** Position each candle and its rose base on the dinner table, placing the tall candle in the center and surrounding it with the others.

# harvest time and thanksgiving
## candle pot

*This very simple and traditional idea using a terra cotta plant pot to hold a candle makes a rich setting for a harvest and Thanksgiving table decoration. Surround the pot with all the delights from this time of year – fruits and vegetables, preserves and small pies.*

### you will need

- **glue gun**
- **cinnamon sticks**
- **terra cotta plant pot**
- **thick natural colored candle**
- **floral foam**
- **scissors or craft knife**
- **bay leaves**
- **wheat stalks**
- **fir cones**
- **natural string**

**o n e** Using a hot glue gun, glue the cinnamon sticks around the outside of the plant pot. Space them out evenly and position them upright so that they stand above the edge of the pot.

**t w o** Place the candle in the center of the pot. Cut the floral foam to fit around the candle to secure it in place – you may have to cut the floral foam into little pieces and slot them in wherever they fit. Position the pieces until the candle stands quite firmly on its own, without moving.

**three** Position the bay leaves in and around the outside edges of the floral foam so that they sit in the plant pot with their tops pushed out.

**four** Trim the wheat to a suitable height, so that it doesn't stand too high next to the candle. It should be pushed into the floral foam between the candle and bay leaves. Fill the remaining floral foam with wheat.

**five** Tie the fir cones onto a long length of string. Wind the string around the cinnamon sticks.

*"My candle burns at both ends;*
*It will not last the night;*
*But ah, my foes, and oh, my friends –*
*It gives a lovely light."*

**EDNA ST. VINCENT MILLAY** "A FEW FIGS FROM THISTLES" (1920)

**outdoor tin lanterns** Tin lanterns, candlesticks, and a variety of old glass bottles and vases make perfect holders

for candles, especially if they look well used. Lanterns and vases are great for outdoors as the flame of the candle is

protected by the surround of its holder, so they seldom go out.

# christmas table centerpiece

*A traditional eye-catching Christmas table centerpiece with holly and berries is a must for this special festive dinner. It is best to use fresh holly and berries. If you cannot get fresh berries use fir cones instead.*

**you will need**

**florist wire**

**three red candles**

**floral foam block**

**scissors or craft knife**

**twig ring**

**old, large plate**

**holly**

**wire cutters**

**berries**

**o n e** Wind a length of florist wire around the base of each candle. Wrap the wire around the entire candle once, twist the sides together, and then point the ends of the wire downward.

**t h r e e** Attach the wired candles into the floral foam center, pushing them deep into it, so that they are secure and upright.

**t w o** Cut the floral foam block to fit inside the twig ring. Place the floral foam inside the ring, and place both onto the plate.

**four** Trim pieces of holly with the wire cutters. Wind the holly into position around the wreath and into the floral foam.

**five** Fill in the exposed floral foam with more holly leaves, pushed into the floral foam.

**six** Fill in the remaining gaps and base of each candle with berries.

**Christmas candles** Gold globe-shaped candles are placed in tulip candle holders and look perfect next to the cherub

candles. Place a few small branches of holly with berries and a selection of nuts for a luxurious table decoration.

"*Night's candles are burnt out, and jocund day stands tiptoe on the misty mountain tops.*"

**SHAKESPEARE** ROMEO AND JULIET ACT 3, SC.5 I.9.

# floating candle display

*Floating candles can look fantastic alight in a bowl of water, however, they can look even more stunning when incorporated into a themed display. An outdoor display can consist of items collected from the beach and kept as mementos of your vacation, like shells, pebbles, washed up seaweed, and starfish.*

**you will need**

**starfish**

**seaweed**

**sheet of old paper**

**silver spray paint**

**polyurethane varnish**

**paintbrush**

**large glass bowl**

**real and colored glass pebbles**

**shells**

**jug of water**

**silver glitter**

**small shaped candles, such as star and ball shapes**

**o n e**  Place the starfish and seaweed in a well ventilated area on a sheet of old paper. Spray paint them with silver paint. Keep the can at least 6 inches away from the surface of the objects that are to be sprayed, and allow a fine mist to coat them. They don't have to be covered very smoothly, they look good if the paint is uneven.

**t h r e e**  Take the large glass bowl and line the bottom and sides with a selection of real and glass pebbles, mixing them so that you have an assortment of colors and textures. Add the occasional small shell with a mother of pearl sheen to it, to add even more interest.

**t w o**  Once the paint has dried, varnish the starfish to preserve them and to stop them from smelling. Do not varnish the seaweed as it will disintegrate.

**four** Place the filled glass bowl onto the center of the table. Pile up more shells, the starfish, and seaweed around the outside of the bowl. Sprinkle some sand around the base of the bowl, if liked.

**five** Pour the water into the bowl on top of the pebbles and shells. Sprinkle a little silver glitter onto the surface of the water.

**six** Float the small shaped candles in the bowl and light.

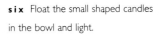

**seaside display** Floating candles in a large bowl of water can be very atmospheric. Add to that a flavor of the seaside

with shells, starfish, seaweed, and pebbles collected from walks along the beach, to make your table candle display a

memento of vacations gone by. Add a touch of sparkle with silver paint and glitter.

"*How sweet the moonlight sleeps upon this bank.*"

**SHAKESPEARE** THE MERCHANT OF VENICE ACT 5 SC. I, I.54

# wedding table candles

*A frothy white display with silk, sheer ribbons, and special silver candles is perfect for a wedding table. Although this one is quite small and informal, the basic principles of the design can be used for a larger and more formal centerpiece, using more candles and a tiered cake stand.*

**length of white habitué silk**

**scissors**

**fresh white lilies**

**cut glass cake stand**

**silver paper leaves**

**adhesive gum**

**paraffin wax pellets**

**one large white pillar candle**

**four thin spiral candles**

**four small nova candles**

**sheer white ribbon**

**silver candies**

**wire cutters**

**o n e** Cut a length of white silk, long enough to wrap around the cake stand base twice, and half as wide. Wind the silk around itself loosely to give it a soft rope-like shape. Now wrap the silk around the cake stand base, tuck in the ends and fluff out the silk if necessary.

**t w o** Cut the open lilies from their stems, leaving the leaves around the flower heads. Gently push the lily heads into the silk, at even intervals around the cake stand.

**three** Cut the stems off the silver paper leaves. Using the adhesive gum, stick the leaves around the outside edge of the cake stand. If the cake stand has scalloped edges, use the pattern as a guide for the placement of the leaves.

**four** Melt a little wax into the center of the cake stand plate. Place the large pillar candle into position, securing it with the melted wax. Alternately, position the spiral and small nova candles around the edge, securing with melted wax.

**five** Cut various lengths of the sheer white ribbon, with diagonal cuts at the ends. Tie them into generous single and double bows, leaving long trailing ends. Put them into position around the candles on the cake stand.

**s e v e n** Cut the closed lilies and lily buds from their stems, leaving the leaves around the flower heads. Scatter them decoratively around the cake stand display.

**s i x** Scatter the silver candies on the cake stand, and around the white ribbon bows. Rearrange the trails of the ribbons to show the candies and bows if necessary.

# individual candle pots
## wedding table

*A nice idea for the smaller and more intimate wedding guest table is an individual silver leafed pot containing a candle.*

**you will need**

small terra cotta plant pot

light blue acrylic or latex paint

paintbrushes

all-purpose adhesive glue

silver leaf

floral foam

craft knife

white candle

small flowers

**one** Paint a small terra cotta pot with a couple of coats of light blue paint. Two or three coats should be ideal for a smooth and even finish.

**two** Once the paint on the pot has dried, paint a layer of glue all over the surface. Allow it to almost dry, until it is just sticky.

**three** Carefully lay sheets of silver leaf onto the sticky surface and gently press into place. Don't worry if pieces of silver leaf come away from the surface as the surface will be distressed.

**four** Using a large soft paintbrush, gently brush away the excess silver leaf in places. Use your fingernail to scrape away the silver to reveal the blue underneath.

**five** Cut a piece of floral foam to fit inside the pot.

**seven** Cover the floral foam with small flowers.

**six** Gently push the candle into the center of the pot.

# CANDLEHOLDERS AND
## *containers*

THERE ARE SO MANY VARIETIES OF CANDLEHOLDERS AND CONTAINERS TO CHOOSE FROM, THE CHOICE IS

OFTEN OVERWHELMING. IN FACT, OFTEN A CANDLESTICK OR HOLDER IS BOUGHT BEFORE THE CANDLES AS

THEY ARE A DECORATIVE CRAFT WITHIN THEMSELVES, MADE FROM ALL KINDS OF MATERIALS, SUCH AS

TERRA COTTA, MARBLE, METAL, AND PLASTICS.

THIS SELECTION OF PROJECTS KEEPS TO THE NATURAL LOOK OF THE CANDLES, AND SOMETIMES GIVES THE

NATURAL INGREDIENTS A COLOR BOOST. FOR EXAMPLE, THE TERRA COTTA POTS HAVE BEEN DECORATED IN

VIBRANT COLORS AND THE GLASS CONTAINERS HAVE BEEN PAINTED IN BRIGHT COLORS, TOO. WHEREAS,

THE PEBBLE AND METAL HOLDERS HAVE BEEN LEFT NATURAL.

# painted terra cotta pots

*Garden candles often come in their own containers, like patio candles in buckets, garden torches in bowls or terra cotta pots. The pots used here have a ridged surface, but a plain pot would work just as well. As terra cotta works with bright acrylic paints so well, they inspired a Mexican look using acid colors along the ridges. For a striking effect, paint lots of pots different colors and position them round the room or on the patio.*

### you will need

**terra cotta garden candle pots**

**purple, lime green, yellow, and pink acrylic paints**

**fine flat paintbrush**

**two** Wash the paintbrush thoroughly. Fill in the remaining sections in yellow and pink paint, again working in long slow movements with the paintbrush for the straight lines. As you have been working freehand, some edges may be a little uneven, so touch up all the edges when the paint has dried. Paint the top edge rim over to the candle wax in yellow to give a strong finish.

**one** If the pots you have aren't ridged, make equally spaced lines around the pot. Using the purple and green paints first, fill in the top two sections. Paint in long smooth strokes to achieve a straight line. Skip two sections, then fill in the next two in purple and green.

# metal lanterns and buckets

*I bought some tiny galvanized buckets measuring only 3 inches in height and discovered that tea lights slotted into them perfectly. Together with a number of little tin lanterns with stars cut from them, made specifically for candles, they look very special hung from the branches of a tree, with strands of pebbles and bells.*

**o n e** Choose a selection of small rounded pebbles. Apply glue with a glue gun around each pebble, then wind the natural string around the pebble to secure it. Leave about 6 inches at one end.

**t w o** Leaving a space on the string between pebbles, wind another pebble on to the string and repeat until you have length of about 15 inches. String five or six lengths of pebbles together.

**three** On the end of each length, attach a little round bell by threading the string through the bell loop and tying securely.

**four** Cut 6–inch lengths of florist wire and hook them through the bucket handles. Thread them with string, this will prevent the string from coming into close contact with the flame.

**five** Loop various lengths of natural string through the handles of the buckets and lanterns. Hang them onto a tree if possible. Hang the pebble and bell strings in between each one. Place tea lights in the buckets and lanterns.

# painted glass candleholders

*Glass has always been popular for candlesticks and holders, in various thicknesses, colors, and textures. Rich stained glass can be recreated inexpensively, using plain drinking glasses and jars, with glass paints and relief outliners.*

### you will need

**paper**

**pencils**

**gold and lead colored glass outliner**

**paper towels**

**glass jars and plain drinking glasses**

**soft paintbrush**

**blue, green, red, orange, turquoise glass paints**

**brush cleaner**

**three** The outliner works as a barrier for the glass paint, which tends to seep and spread really quickly. By using the outliner, the paint will stay within this outline. Apply the paint little by little, using one color for the motifs and another for the background.

**one** Draw your designs on paper first. The simpler motifs like suns, moons, and stars are ideal as it is difficult to paint a perfect motif on a rounded surface.

**two** Using the glass outliner, pipe the motifs on to the glass or jar. Draw in long and smooth motions as the outliner tends to blob if you stop and start. If you make a mistake, just wipe it off with paper towels. Allow to dry, according to the manufacturer's instructions.

# using one color

**one** Apply the glass paint to the entire surface of the drinking glass or jar with a soft brush. Leave to dry and then add another layer.

**two** Once the glass paint has dried, draw the outline for the motifs directly onto the glass.

*"Twinkle, twinkle, little star,*
*How I wonder what you are!"*

**A. TAYLOR AND J. TAYLOR** "THE STAR"

**candles in an oval shaped basket** An easy storage idea for a multitude of candles is simply laying them in a long basket. Keep a pile of candles together in

similar colors, so that they look just as attractive unlit as they do lit. To make the larger twisted candle, a dipped candle is flattened and twisted while still quite

malleable. It is then redipped in different colors to give a stripy effect.

# cutwork candle shade

*Candle shades are surprisingly expensive to buy, yet so simple and quick to make. Brass holders to hold the shade in place above the flame are available in most department stores. Always use this type of holder with the candle shade. The inspiration behind these shades came from silhouettes of leaves and flowers, echoing the natural beauty and simplicity of the handmade paper. Always use candle shades with particular care.*

**you will need**

**tracing paper**

**sheet of thin card**

**natural handmade paper**

**craft knife**

**cutting mat**

**paintbrush**

**glue**

**paper clips**

**brass shade holders**

**one** Trace the template on page 124 – this is the actual size of a regular candle shade so there is no need to enlarge or reduce it. Trace it onto a sheet of thin card and cut out, to create a template.

**two** Draw around the card template onto the natural handmade paper. Cut it out using a sharp craft knife and the cutting mat.

**three** Referring to the leaf templates on pages 124-5, either copy these onto the back of the handmade paper or trace them. Any simple motifs can be used.

you will need

**tracing paper**

**heavy paper**

**pencil**

**craft knife or scissors**

**cutting mat**

**large needle**

**paintbrush**

**glue**

**paper clips**

**o n e**  Trace a scalloped edged candle shade from the template on page 125. Trace it onto the heavy paper and cut out the candle shade.

**t w o**  On the reverse of the shade, draw a series of oak leaf shapes with a pencil. Draw them on at irregular angles to make it look as if the leaves are floating down the shade.

**t h r e e**  Place the candle shade, with the drawings facing up, on the cutting mat. Pierce along the pencil lines with the large needle, quite close together. Also pierce along the top and lower edges of the shade.

**f o u r**  Glue the short edges together to complete the shade, holding the edges together with paper clips until the glue has dried. When the candle is lit, the light will filter through the pierced shapes to make the patterns glow.

**f o u r**  Using the craft knife and cutting mat, carefully cut along the pencil lines. Be extremely careful not to cut the leaf shape out completely, leaving the top and bottom part of the motif attached to the paper.

**f i v e**  Glue the short edges together to complete the shade, holding the edges together with paper clips until the glue has dried. Twist the leaf or flower motifs until they are at right angles to the actual shade, then allow them to fall back slightly. Secure the shade to the brass holder. When the candle is lit inside the shade, the silhouettes will look very striking.

*candleholders and containers*

**101**

# lavender wreath candleholder

*The ever popular lavender wreath has been adapted into a stylish candleholder, providing the fragrance of lavender from your candle even before you begin to burn it. Alternatively, make smaller wreaths and use as individual table settings. Do not let the flame burn down to the level of the lavender as it could catch fire.*

**you will need**

**dried lavender**

**scissors**

**small twig wreath**

**thick altar candle, to fit the wreath**

**one** Trim the dried lavender so that the stems are only 2 inches long. The easiest way to do this is to hold the lavender in bunches and cut a group of them together.

**two** Place the small wreath on a flat work surface. Begin to thread the lavender into and around the wreath by simply pushing the stems into the twisted twigs.

**three** Fill the wreath with lavender so that most of it is covered. The twig wreath doesn't need to be completely covered.

**four** Turn the lavender wreath candleholder upside down and shake it gently, this will make the loose lavender and broken stems fall out. Fill in the gaps with more lavender if necessary. Slot the candle into the center of the wreath.

*candleholders and containers*

**103**

**alter candles in a basket** A selection of large altar candles have been wrapped in various muted wrappings, to give a feel of autumn to them. The thin

candle on the right has been surrounded by long cinnamon sticks, which have been secured with strands of raffia. The candle in the middle is wrapped in brown

paper and tied with paper string and a long, thin strip of corrugated, ridged card. The candle on the left has, again, been wrapped in brown paper and sealed.

"*Look at the stars! look, look up at the skies!*"

G. M. HOPKINS "THE STARLIGHT NIGHT" (1877)

# clay candlestick

*When baked in the oven, this versatile commercial colored oven hardening clay hardens like pottery in a kiln. This clay is available in a variety of colors that can also be mixed together to make new shades. Experiment with different colors and designs to make stylish candlesticks.*

**red and green oven hardening clay**

**wooden board**

**rolling pin**

**wine glass or lid to make a base**

**knife**

**red candle**

**sheet of baking parchment**

**baking tray**

**two** Pinch the outer edges creating a scalloped effect.

**one** Cut a small block of green clay in half. Knead and roll the clay in your hands for several minutes to make it softer and more pliable. Roll out the clay until about ¼ inch thick. Using a small round shape like a wine glass as a guide, cut out a circle.

**three** For the roses, using red clay, roll out a sausage shape. Cut three equal sized small pieces and one longer piece.

**four**  Take the last longer piece of clay and flatten into a small rectangular shape. Roll this up, at a slight angle, to form a little roll. This will make the center of the rose.

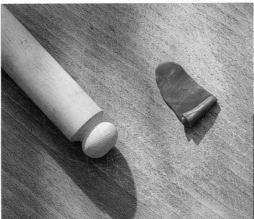

**five**  Roll each smaller piece into a ball. Flatten to make circles, then pinch one end of each circle to form a petal.

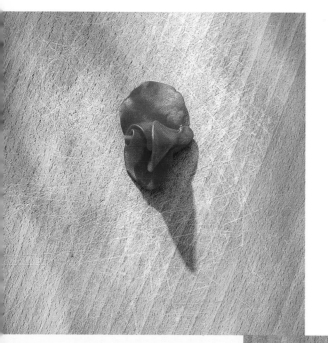

**seven** Repeat the process of making the roses until there are enough to surround the candlestick base, about four or five roses.

**six** Proceed to add the other petals around the center, turning the petals over and adjusting them once they are attached.

**eight** Stand your chosen candle in the center of the green base. Press to mark its place and remove. Attach the roses around the marked position on the green base. Place the candlestick in a preheated oven at 265°F on the middle shelf. Bake for 20–30 minutes. Cool. Position the candle in the center.

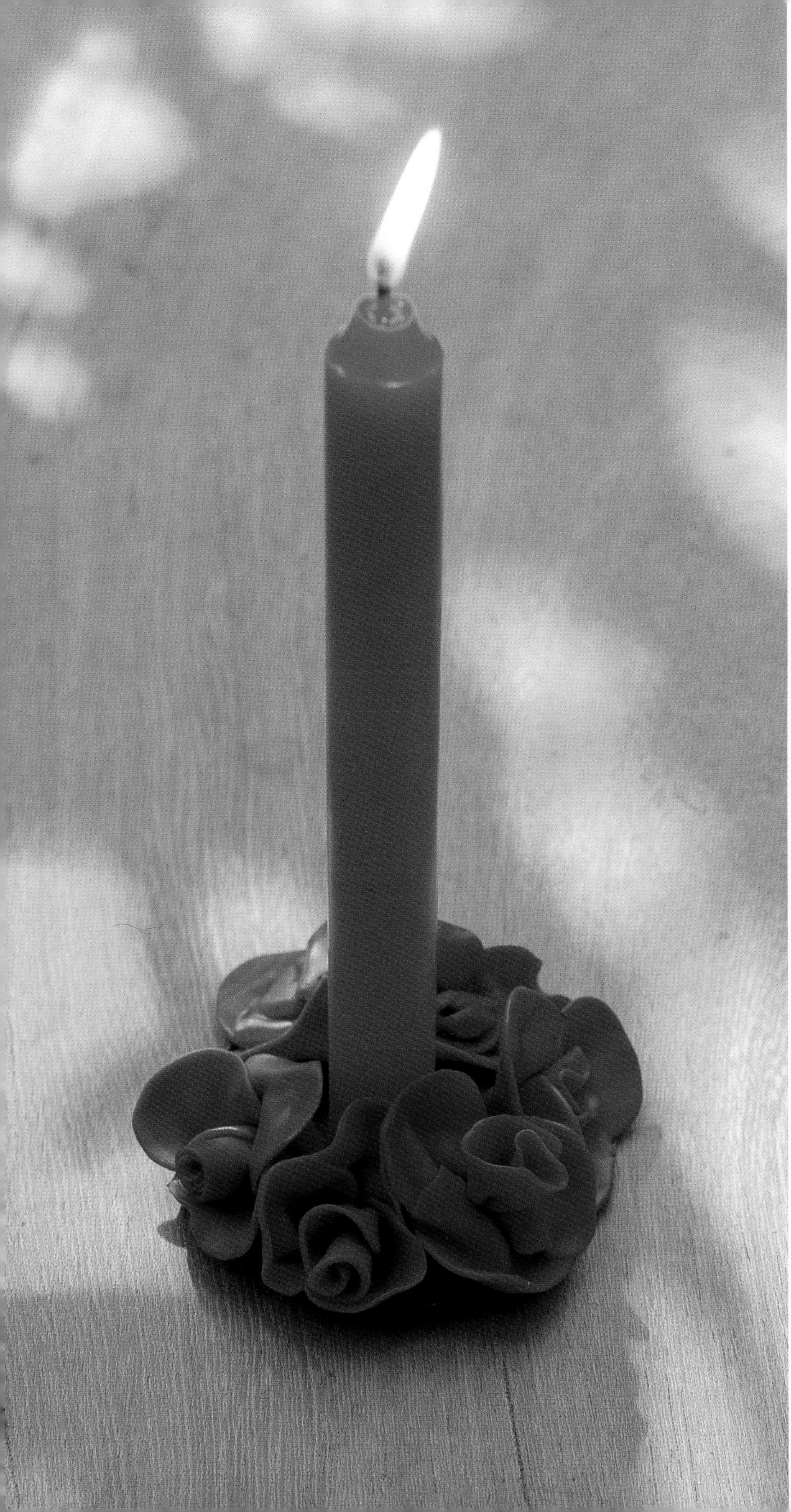

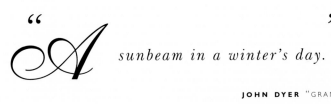 sunbeam in a winter's day.

JOHN DYER "GRANGER HILL" (1726) L.88.

**pink windowsill** A feature has been made of a selection of pink and red candles, placed alongside pink flowers in natural

terra cotta containers tied with ribbons. The swirly pear-shaped candles are quite unusual in their color distribution and

texture, which is really noticeable when they stand next to plain single colored pillar candles.

# pebble and wire candleholder

*This is an extremely simple, natural yet elegant candleholder for a single candle. Large smooth pebbles like the ones found washed up on the beach are the best ones to use for this project.*

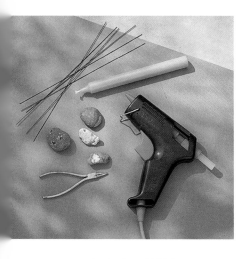

**you will need**

**four large pebbles**

**glue gun**

**florist wire**

**round nosed pliers**

**one green candle**

**o n e**  Take one of the large pebbles and carefully squeeze glue around it in a thin line.

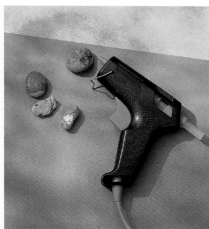

**t w o**  Take a piece of florist wire and carefully wind half of it around the pebble where it has been glued. Ensure that the unwound wire is straight and upright. Work quickly as the glue dries very fast.

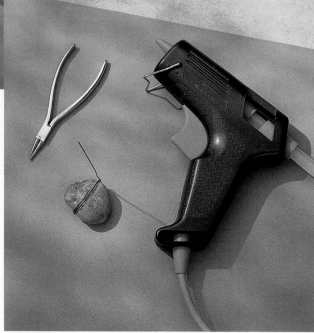

*candleholders and containers*

**four** Stand the four wires together, using the pebbles as the base, and place the candle in the middle to measure for the size of the holder.

**five** Apply glue to the base of each piece of wire, where it leaves the pebble. Wind a further length of florist wire around the candle, encompassing the upright wires and pushing the bottom ring into the glued areas.

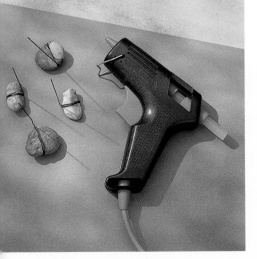

**three** Repeat the process with all four pebbles.

# pumpkin lanterns

*To make a perfect Halloween, pumpkin lanterns are a must. Not only with scary faces for the children but with more sophisticated engravings made for everyone. Pumpkins look amazing with candles inside them as the orange skin provides a luxurious glow.*

**two** Using a large spoon, scoop out the pumpkin seeds and strands from inside the pumpkin skin.

**you will need**

**pumpkin**

**sharp knife**

**large spoon**

**fine marker pen**

**cutting tool**

**sharp craft knife**

**small candle**

**one** Slice the top of the pumpkin with the knife. Cut it about 2 inches from the stem, cutting at a slight downwards angle, work around the top gently until it comes loose. Reserve the top.

**three** Scrape out the insides of the pumpkin. Take as much as you possibly can, because it is easier to carve the pumpkin when the skin is thinner. About ¾ inch is the ideal thickness. Refrigerate the pumpkin flesh for use in cooking.

**five** Using the cutting tool first, score along the curly and wavy lines. Push the tool into the pumpkin at a 45 degree angle and work away from yourself, pushing out strips of pumpkin as you work. This should score the skin, but not penetrate it.

**four** Using the template on page 122 as a guide, carefully draw the design onto the pumpkin skin. Use the lines of the pumpkin to assist with the design of the pattern.

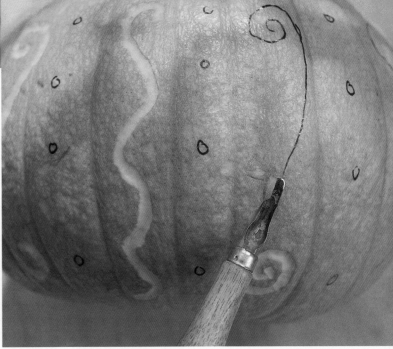

**six** Carefully push the cutting tool into the marks for the tiny holes and twist so that it penetrates the skin and removes tiny rounds of pumpkin. Do this on all the places marked for the holes.

**seven** Using a very sharp craft knife, cut out the marked wavy lines which have already been scored by the cutting tool to make it easier.

**eight** Mark dots around the top of the pumpkin at equal intervals. Use the cutting tool as in step six, to remove tiny rounds to produce the holes.

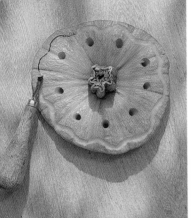

**n i n e** Using the cutting tool, score
a wavy line around the base of the
lid. Secure a candle inside the
decorated pumpkin and replace the
lid, if liked.

**fruit and vegetables** A selection of fruit and vegetables have been carefully hollowed out and with a little imagination

transformed into fantastic candleholders. Tea lights look perfect in the bell of peppers while small beeswax and pillar candles

look elegant in the larger vegetables. These holders are shown as a project on page 120.

" *No man, when he hath lighted a candle, putteth it in a secret place, neither under a bushel.* "

ST. LUKE CH. II, V. 33

# fruit and vegetable
## candleholders

*A wide variety of fruits and vegetables can very easily be transformed into candleholders with the help of a small sharp knife and a little imagination. However, as the fruit and vegetables are fresh you must note that they will not last for more than a couple of days and, in many cases, only one day.*

### eggplant

Simply use an apple corer to twist out rounds of eggplant flesh. Place candles into the holes.

### green and red bell peppers

Slice the top off the pepper, taking the stem and seeds with it. Scoop out any remaining seeds. Cut away the white sections along the insides. Place the candle into the empty pepper.

### savoy cabbage

An ornamental cabbage plant looks fantastic as a candleholder. Just part, remove or fold back the center leaves until the cavity is large enough for the candle.

### squash

Use the same principle for squash as for the eggplant. Score smaller holes and then place several plain candles into the vegetable.

### apples and oranges

Using an apple corer, core an apple and fit in a thin candle. For an orange, use a sharp fruit knife to make a cavity to fit a candle.

### acorn squash

These vegetables have a really interesting shape. Cut the top off the squash, removing the seeds, then you will notice the rounded star shape top edge. Insert a candle into the cavity.

# lates

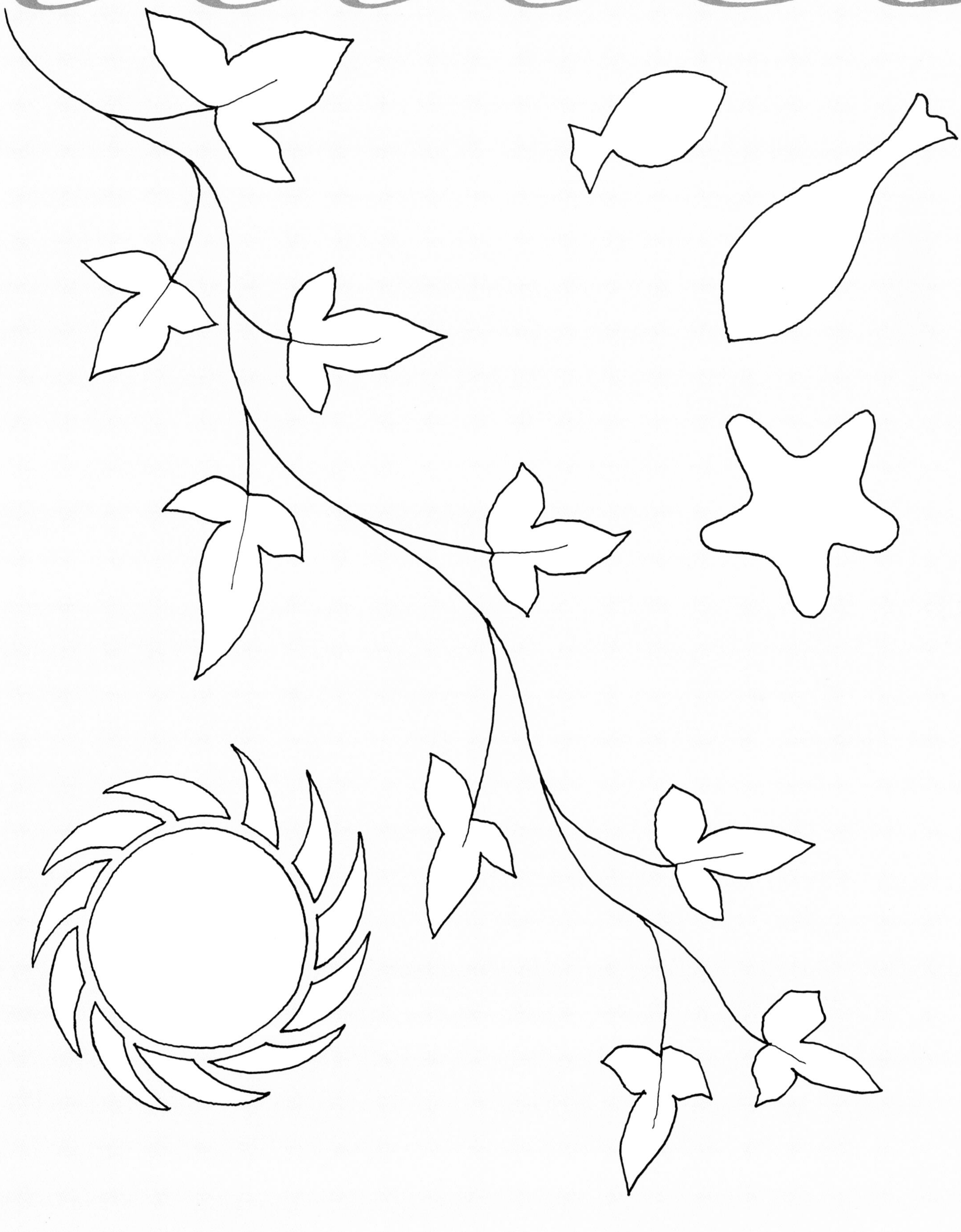

# acknowledgements

*the author, stylist, and publishers would like to thank the following for their generous help in both supplying information and goods.*

SUPPLIERS

United States

**BARKER ENTERPRISES, INC**
15106 10th Avenue, SW
Seattle, WA 98166
(206) 244 1870
*candlemaking supplies including dyes, wax and candle molds*

**CANDLECHEM CO**
PO Box 705
Randolph, MA 02368
(617) 986 7541
*free catalog on request*

**CANDLESTICK**
2444 Broadway
New York, NY 10024
(212) 787 5444
*selection of classic and novelty candles. Wax, dyes and molds also available*

**POTTERY BARN**
Mail Order Department
PO Box 7044
San Francisco, CA 94120-7044
(800) 922 5507
*mail order catalog. Also stores in major cities nation-wide*

United Kingdom

**FRED ALDOUS**
PO Box 135
137 Lever Street
Manchester M60 1UX
0161-236 2477
*mail order craft suppliers*

**CANDLE MAKERS SUPPLIES**
28 Blythe Road
London W14 0HA
0171-602 4031/2
*for candle making equipment and advice*

**THE CANDLES SHOP**
30 The Market
Covent Garden
London WC2E 8RE
0171-836 9815
*for candles*

**INSCRIBE LTD**
The Woolmer Industrial Estate
Bordon
Hampshire GU35 9QE
01420 475747
*for fimo, colored pencils and other craft items*

**KIRKER GREER & CO**
Belvedere Road
Burnham-on-Crouch
Essex CM0 8AJ
01621 784647
*beeswax candles in natural and cream colors*

**PETER NORRIS**
0181-769 5054
*supplier of beeswax and beeswax candles*

**PHILIP & TACEY**
North Way
Andover
Hampshire SP10 5BA
01264 332171
*for glass paint and outliner*

**PLASTI-KOTE**
London Road Industrial Estate
Sawston
Cambridge CB2 4TR
*supplier of metallic and acrylic spray paints*

**POINT À LA LIGNE**
Michael Johnson (Ceramics) Ltd
81 Kingsgate Road
London NW6 4JY
0171-624 2493
*candles, accessories, sticks*

**PRICES CANDLES**
110 York Road
Battersea
London SW11 3RU
0171-228 3345
*for candles, holders, and shades*

Australia

**THE CRAFT COMPANY**
272 Victoria Avenue
Chatswood NSW 2067
(02) 413 1781
*waxes, dyes, wicks and molds*

**JANET'S ART SUPPLIES**
145 Victoria Avenue
Chatswood NSW 2067
(02) 417 8572
*candlemaking kits*

**JOHN L. GUILFOYLE PTY LTD**
772 Boundary Road
Darra QLO 4076
(07) 375 3677
*beeswax sheets, natural and colored, wicks*

# index